EATING
FRACTIONS

FOR CHRIS

Design by Bruce McMillan
Art direction by Claire Counihan
Text set in Optima and Optima Medium
Color separations by Color Dot
First edition printed and bound by Horowitz/Rae

Library of Congress Cataloging-in-Publication Data
McMillan, Bruce.
Eating fractions/photo-illustrated by Bruce McMillan.
p.   cm.
Summary: Food is cut into halves, thirds,
and fourths to illustrate how parts make a whole.
Recipes included.
ISBN 0-590-43770-4
1. Fractions—Juvenile literature. [1. Fractions.]
I. Title. QA117.M26 1991 513.2'6—dc20
90-9139 CIP AC

12 11 10 9 8 7 6 5 4 3   2 3 4 5 6/9
Printed in the U.S.A.   36
First Scholastic printing, September 1991

EATING FRACTIONS

Cooked, Written, Drafted, and Photo-illustrated by

Bruce McMillan

 SCHOLASTIC INC. • New York

WHOLE

1

HALVES

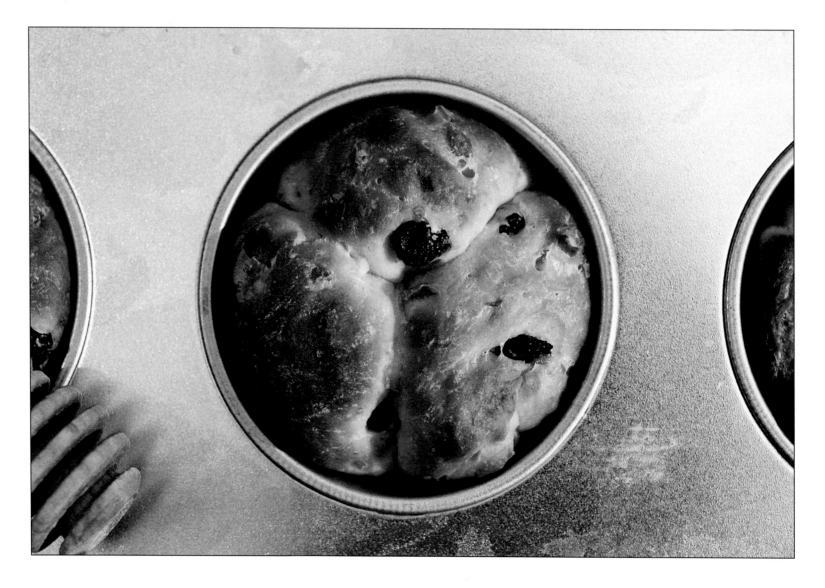

WHOLE

1

THIRDS

WHOLE

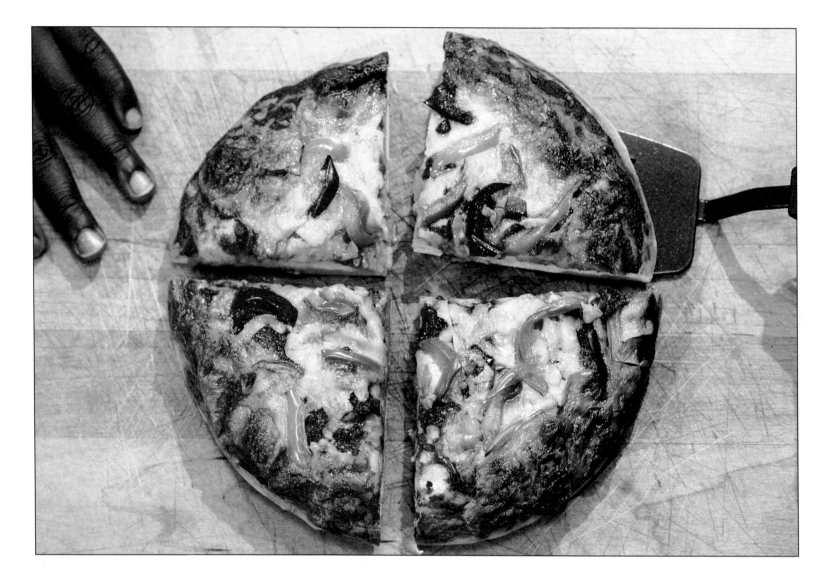

FOURTHS

WHOLE

1

HALVES

WHOLE

THIRDS

WHOLE

FOURTHS

¼ ¼ ¼ ¼

BRUCE'S CLOVERLEAF RABBIT ROLLS

Rolls with carrots in them!

Makes 15 rolls

¼ cup warm water (105°-115°F)	3⅛ cups flour
1 tbsp (packet) active dry yeast	¾ cup cooked carrots, sliced
⅞ cup warm milk (105°-115°F)	⅓ cup raisins
1 tbsp sugar	⅓ cup almonds
½ tbsp salt	vegetable oil
1½ tbsp margarine	honey

Measure warm water into a food processor (regular blade). Sprinkle in yeast. Run until dissolved. Add warm milk, sugar, salt, margarine, and 1 cup of the flour. Run for 1 minute until smooth. Change processor blade to dough blade. Add ½ cup flour. Run for 1 minute. Add raisins, almonds, and 1⅝ cups of flour. Run for 3 minutes. Add carrots and run until the carrots are chopped and thoroughly mixed with dough. (Or, if kneading by hand, knead for 10 minutes while slowly adding the flour. Then mix in nuts, raisins, and chopped carrots.)

Place dough in a greased bowl, cover with wax paper, and let it rise in a warm place for at least 20 minutes. Grease muffin pans for 15 muffins.

Remove wax paper and punch down dough. Divide dough into thirds. Roll out each third into a solid tube. Cut each length into 15 equal pieces. Place 3 pieces, flat side up, in each muffin holder. Brush with vegetable oil and cover with wax paper. Refrigerate for 2–24 hours.

When ready to bake, uncover rolls and let them stand for 30 minutes at room temperature. Bake at 400°F for 15–20 minutes, or until golden-brown. Drizzle with honey.

BRUCE'S PEPPER PIZZA PIE

Makes two 6" pizzas or one 12" pizza

3 tbsp warm water (105°-115°F)	1 cup grated mozzarella cheese
½ tbsp (½ packet) active dry yeast	2 tsp oregano
2 cups flour	⅓ green pepper, sliced
2 tbsp olive oil	⅓ red pepper, sliced
1 tsp salt	⅓ yellow pepper, sliced
6 oz can tomato paste	white cornmeal

Measure warm water into a food processor (dough blade). Sprinkle in yeast. Run until dissolved. Add flour, 1 tbsp olive oil, and salt. Run for 3 minutes until dough is smooth. Place dough in an oiled bowl, cover with wax paper, and place in a warm place for 2 hours until it has doubled in bulk.

Punch down dough, divide in two. On a flour-sprinkled surface, and using a rolling pin, roll each ball out into a 6" circle. Or, if you're adventuresome, spin-toss the dough into a pizza shape. Lightly sprinkle each pizza pan with white cornmeal. Place the flat circle of dough onto the pan and prick all over with a fork.

Spoon 3 oz of tomato paste onto each pizza and spread evenly with a rubber spatula. Sprinkle ½ cup mozzarella cheese and 1 tsp oregano on each pizza. Drizzle each with ½ tbsp olive oil. Cover evenly with the different-colored peppers. Let stand for 10 minutes. Preheat oven to 400°F.

Bake for 25 minutes or until crust is light brown.

Children can:
Measure the fractional quantities of the ingredients.
Pour the mixture into four bowls, the four fractional
parts of the set.

Children can:
Measure the fractional quantities of the ingredients.
Divide the quart of berries in half.

BRUCE'S WIGGLE PEAR SALAD

Makes 4 servings

1 envelope unflavored gelatin	4 tbsp sugar
2 16 oz cans of pear halves <u>in</u> <u>pear juice</u>	2 tbsp lime juice concentrate green food coloring
water	(optional)
4 oz cream cheese	leaf lettuce

Drain pear juice into 2-cup measuring cup. Add enough water to make 2 cups. In a medium bowl, mix the gelatin with ½ cup of the pear juice/water. Let it stand. Boil 1 cup of the pear juice/water and pour into the bowl, dissolving the gelatin completely. Add 4 tbsp of sugar and dissolve it. Add 2 tbsp lime juice concentrate, and a drop of green food coloring (if you wish). Add the remaining ½ cup of pear juice/water, and pour the mixture into a blender. Add the cream cheese and blend at high speed for 1 minute.

Place pear halves in four small bowls. Pour the liquid mixture into each bowl, covering the pears. Refrigerate until firm and serve on a bed of leaf lettuce.

BRUCE'S FRESH STRAWBERRY PIE

Makes one 8" pie shell
(for the pie size seen in this book,
use two 6" springform pans, and 1½ times this recipe)

PIE CRUST

1½ cups flour	¼ cup vegetable shortening
¼ tsp salt	4 tbsp cold vinegar
¼ cup margarine	

Preheat oven to 425°F. Mix salt into flour. Add margarine and shortening. Mix with a fork or pastry blender, or cut dough in a crisscross slicing motion with two knives until it's the size of tiny peas. Sprinkle the cold vinegar, 1 tbsp at a time, over the mixture four times while doing this. Do not overdo this mixing or the dough will be tough. Place the dough onto wax paper. Lay another piece of wax paper over this and roll with a rolling pin. Peel back top paper. Lay pie plate upside down on the flat dough. Turn everything over, press the dough onto the plate, and peel back the remaining paper. Fill the shell with dried beans (to hold it down when cooking—pour the beans out after cooking and save them for the next pie). Bake for 15 minutes. Cool.

STRAWBERRY FILLING

4 cups (1 quart) fresh strawberries or whole, unsweetened frozen berries, thawed	1 cup sugar 3 tbsp cornstarch

Slice half the berries. Crush the remaining berries. Add cornstarch and sugar to the crushed berries. Cook the crushed berries in a saucepan until the mixture begins to boil. Pour sliced berries into cooled pie shell. Then, pour hot crushed berry mixture into the pie shell. Let it cool.

Eating Fractions is a story about a tasty meal shared by two youngsters and their dog. It's also an introduction to the mathematical concept of fractions. It shows fractions as parts of a whole. Using the simplest fractional units of halves, thirds, and fourths, this book illustrates subtractive fractions—dividing and taking away parts of the whole. While young readers enjoy the activities of the story's characters, they will be challenged to develop and use mathematical skills—comparing, seeing relationships, matching, logic, and identifying fractional parts. The sequence of halves, thirds, and fourths, is repeated in this book so that the skills are reinforced. An extension of fractional thinking can be made by cooking these recipes with youngsters. Additive fractions can be demonstrated as the children measure ingredients. Adults and children cannot only cook up a math lesson together, they can eat it too.

The recipes used, unique to this book, are my variations on tried-and-true standards. They include some cooking tips I've picked up. For example, once, when I ate a pie baked by an elderly lady, I asked her what the secret was for such a tender crust. She told me that she used vinegar instead of water. I've been using vinegar ever since. The foods in the recipes are balanced for nutrition, and include all the basic food groups. Although it wasn't planned, it's a meatless meal. By using foods not at the top of the food chain we reduce the stress on the resources of our planet.

Erin Mallat and Melvin Chace first met each other the day we began taking pictures, and fortunately enjoyed each other's company. A kindergarten teacher, Bev Olean, had suggested Erin as "a character with freckles who might be fun for your book." I'd already met Melvin when I'd photographed his brother for a previous book, *One Sun*. I outfitted Erin and Melvin, each with a duplicate set of new, color-coordinated clothes. This allowed for mishaps like spills and stains. Their mothers, Kathy Mallat and Jeanne Chace, were invaluable aides at every photo session.

Lillie, the strawberry pie-eating dog, is owned and cared for by veterinarian Dr. Craig Holbrook. When I'm photographing a book, I always ask my local veterinarians for suggestions about where I can locate cooperative animals with personality. This time, one of the three veterinarian partners and the receptionist replied without hesitating, "Dr. Holbrook's dog, Lillie." At first I thought that they

just wanted to have their friend's dog in a book. But they weren't exaggerating when they said that Lillie is the cutest and most personable dog that they know.

Eating Fractions was photo-illustrated using a Nikon F4 with 50mm AF, 55mm micro AF, 85mm AF, 105mm AI, and 180mm AF Nikkor lenses. The interior lighting was balanced with the available daylight at the windows. To match the natural daylight color temperature, the lighting consisted of an on-camera trip flash with two off-camera bare-bulb flash units and one dichroic quartz light. To match the warmth of normal interior incandescent lighting, two quartz lights were used to warm the colors slightly. The flash allowed the action to freeze, while the quartz lighting allowed the action to blur slightly and show movement. The film used was Kodachrome 64, processed by Kodalux.

Bruce McMillan

DATE DUE

AG 4 '92		
MAY 1 3 '94		
FEB 1 2 2001		
AUG 6 2003		
FEB 1 9 2004		
MAR 4 2004		

DEMCO 38-297